IMAGES
of America

EASLEY

IMAGES
of America

EASLEY

Brantli Jane Owens

ARCADIA
PUBLISHING

Published by Arcadia Publishing
Charleston SC, Chicago IL, Portsmouth NH, San Francisco CA

Library of Congress Catalog Card Number: 2008931964

For all general information contact Arcadia Publishing at:
Telephone 843-853-2070
Fax 843-853-0044
E-mail sales@arcadiapublishing.com
For customer service and orders:
Toll-Free 1-888-313-2665

Visit us on the Internet at www.arcadiapublishing.com

*To my family: J. B. "Pa" Owens and "Grandma Ellen" A. Owens;
Steve A. Owens, my daddy; Cindy S. Owens, my mama;
and Alex Owens, my brother and best friend.*

CONTENTS

ACKNOWLEDGMENTS

The Greater Easley Chamber of Commerce pulled together to provide the contacts, information, and history necessary to get this project off the ground. If it weren't for the members' hard work, this book may not have been written. The Pickens County Library System and the Pendleton District Historical Commission—the keepers of our history—were more than generous with their time and information.

I also wish to thank Arcadia Publishing and especially Maggie Bullwinkel for her patience and understanding during a time of great turmoil. Truly, and in so many ways, had it not been for her, this book would not have been. The *Easley Progress* and *Pickens Sentinel* were of great assistance as well.

The book committee is Kent Dykes, Vicki Fletcher, Jack Ragsdale, Jimmy Stewart, and Dub Fortner. You will always have my abiding respect for your true concern for our community.

Finally, thanks to all who contributed information or photographs: Mary Robinson, Newell Hester, Lib Oates, Dub Fortner, Angie Sheriff, the Hagood family, the Owens family, "Slick" Magah, Marie May, Cam Surrett, and the innumerable folks with anecdotes and stories too many to mention here.

INTRODUCTION

As the country recovered from the Civil War, two men with a pioneering spirit and a vision of a promising future picked a largely uninhabited tract of land in the picturesque foothills of the Blue Ridge Mountains to be the birthplace of their dreams and what would eventually become Easley, South Carolina. In present-day Pickens County, a few farming families were scattered across a small portion of the Upstate, in what had been Cherokee country, in a loose conglomeration then known as Pickensville, when Gen. William King Easley proposed that a single rail line be routed through the land north of the headwaters of 18 Mile Creek. General Easley, an attorney for the Atlanta and Charlotte Air Line Company, rallied citizens of the county to offer the railway company $100,000 in bonds in exchange for the privilege of access to the railroad and a depot that was the lifeline of American commerce and communication.

As the Industrial Revolution surged, the rail became all-important in the expansion and growth of America. To have such access to the railway meant having a closer connection to the burgeoning industry and major cities, inducing an almost indescribable economic and cultural impact on the citizenry of the area, as General Easley well knew. He was not the only person to see the potential. Excited by the possibilities, Robert Elliott Holcombe grew impatient for the railroad company to build a depot, so in 1873, he offered to finance, build, and donate a depot to the rail company. His offer was accepted, and the depot was built two miles east of the originally proposed location. Holcombe did not stop with the depot; he also constructed a small dwelling and storeroom, in effect becoming the first citizen of Easley. Within months, he and a few others that settled close to the rail surveyed and plotted a 1-square-mile tract of land. They also included plans for businesses, residences, and streets, incorporating them into a small village with the depot at its center. The first use of the soon-to-be Easley depot was greeted by a small but progressive-minded group of residents with an eye toward the future in April 1873. When the state legislature convened in December of that year, a charter encompassing that small square-mile tract of land was applied for, naming the town in honor of General Easley, and it was granted in January 1874. Robert Elliott Holcombe's efforts in creating the town were rewarded when he was named the first agent of the Easley depot and later the first "intendant," or mayor.

With the depot as the town's heart, the railway pumped life into the community by bringing bountiful commerce in the form of the booming textile industry that was so prominent and important to the South. Easley, like other small Southern towns, thrived as the textile trade grew. The first mill, Easley Oil Mill, was built in the late 1800s. It incorporated a cotton gin and established the tremendous role textiles would play in the life of Easley. At the peak of textile commerce, from the 1950s through the 1970s, Easley hosted six of the largest mills in operation in the Upstate. The mills, each with its own village community, provided a vast percentage of jobs in Easley and fostered the growth of a subculture of American society. To be employed at a mill usually meant living in the housing built by the mill, using the company store, and attending the churches and schools that were specific to each community. A large percentage of the citizens of Easley were living on these various mill hills. To this day, older families are remembered by the mill community to which they belonged, and it is not uncommon to hear someone say "so and so is an old mill hill boy" or tell the tales of growing up on the mill hill. Each mill fostered a community that was unique while at the same time interdependent upon each other, as those employed by the mills were loyal to their mill families, as well as the town at large. Volumes of literature have been written recalling this sense of family and community that the ill-fated mills' textile trade created by providing the school in which one studied, the church in which one worshipped, and the neighborhood in which one lived—the very foundation of each soul under the protection of the close-knit mill communities. During the run of the textile industry and the subculture it established, Easley grew in size and population. Unfortunately, textile production in the United States declined and eventually faded almost entirely. The mills began to close one by one, and in 2008, only one of the old mills, the Ellison Plant, was still in operation. That plant, however, was built in the mid-1970s and had no mill village associated with it. The culture of the mill hill has vanished into history, leaving only memories and popular residential redevelopment areas.

With the demise of the primary catalyst of its economy and job market, Easley turned to the retail commerce and growth of the neighboring city of Greenville and Clemson University to support its population. Highway 123, on the south end of Easley, has become a heavily used corridor for commerce and travel. From the 1970s until the late 1990s and into the 21st century, the economic center of Easley shifted to the bypass. As a result, the downtown area and the precious railroad were largely ignored. Clemson University has attracted students and faculty from all over the world. Greenville has grown and is now home to major international corporations such as Michelin and BMW. Easley's perfect central location between the two, as well as the natural beauty of the nearby Blue Ridge Mountains, lavish lakes, and pristine state parks, have allowed the community to continue to not only grow, but to thrive despite the fall of textile manufacturing. The chamber of commerce, the downtown business association, and prominent and active members of the community have initiated the revitalization of the historic downtown area that straddles the railway. Repurposing the buildings that were originally built along the railroad 100 years ago, the heart of Easley is now populated with antique shops, boutiques, restaurants, and loft apartments with a focus on the tourism industry.

Although the trains do not stop in Easley anymore, their whistles can be heard from miles away, reminding us of our past and still contributing to our evolution into the future. The following pages hold dear memories. They are our past, describing the details of what was, unfolding the truth of what is, and giving us the fortitude to discover what may be.

One

It Began with the Railroad

An ageless truth is said
to ride the rails.
In wakes of sparks it
lights the timbers and
as amber streams
of questions
flash and flair,
choices flit from fancy
to mundane;
from what you are, to
what you want to be—
and what you will become.

—Lucille Younger

ROBERT ELLIOTT HOLCOMBE. Although the town was named after Gen. William King Easley, Robert Holcombe was so instrumental in the birth and development of Easley that he is considered to be the "first citizen" of Easley in many ways. A visionary and progressive businessman, Holcombe built the first dwelling, store, and train depot. Along with being a farmer, miller, and auctioneer, he was named the first agent of the depot and the first "intendant," or mayor. Holcombe, who was highly respected and was widely known as "Colonel Holcombe," was also a civic leader as a member of the local Masonic order. Married twice, he was the devoted father of 15 children—six by his first marriage to Caroline Arnold and nine by his second wife, a Miss Bowen. He lived in the town that he was largely responsible for creating until his death on April 9, 1893, at the age of 70. (Photograph courtesy of the Pickens County Library System.)

GEN. WILLIAM KING EASLEY. General Easley was born in Pickens County, which at the time incorporated Pickens and Oconee Counties, on a plantation along the Saluda River. At the age of 33, he was one of the youngest men ever elected to represent the county in the South Carolina Legislature. He and four men from Greenville were chosen to represent the area in a South Carolina Legislature Secession Convention. When the Civil War was declared, he raised a company of cavalry from Pickens and Greenville Counties, and served as a major in the Confederate army. General Easley was instrumental in the establishment of Easley by persuading the rail company to route a line through the area. Returning to his father's home after living in New Orleans for a short time, he became the local attorney for the Atlanta and Charlotte Air Line Company (later to become Southern Railroad). After convincing the citizens of the area to raise and invest $100,000, General Easley represented the county, convincing the company to bring the railroad through this area instead of the earlier contemplated route through Anderson County. (Photograph courtesy of Pickens County Library System.)

HOLCOMBE HOUSE. As a single man, Holcombe lived in a dwelling he built in the original depot. When he married his first wife, Caroline Arnold, he built a larger home. However, the Holcombes only lived in the home for a short time before it was sold. Shown above from left to right are Elias J. Hester, Sarah O'Dell Mauldin, James Benjamin Hester and Sarah Lucetta Hester. (Photograph courtesy of Pickens County Library System.)

THE STOREROOM. The first business in town, before there even was a town, was built by R. E. Holcombe along with the depot. He was anxious to develop commerce in the area and establish a town around the depot and store. Built in 1845, the storeroom paved the way for the downtown business district. (Photograph courtesy of Newell Hester and family.)

THIRD EASLEY DEPOT. Between 1900 and 1911, the third Easley depot was built and was renovated on multiple occasions. The depot went through four incarnations with several renovations made in and around the building to accommodate the changing times, as shown in the photograph above. (Photograph courtesy of Dub Fortner.)

THE FOURTH DEPOT BUILDING. Above is a photograph of the fourth and final depot building, which had been relocated farther east down the tracks toward the Glenwood mill area and was greatly reduced in size. As the years passed, the depot was used less and less, while the downtown business district grew. (Photograph courtesy of Dub Fortner.)

THE PICKENS DOODLE. Not only did the railroad assist in the birth of small towns across the nation, open a safer passage from the East Coast to the West in an entirely new way, and help to foster the textile industry across the South; it also linked the citizens of Easley to its neighboring community of Pickens, South Carolina. Although Easley has historically been the largest community in the county, the city of Pickens is the county seat. Starting with the first 16-mile round-trip between the two towns, the Doodle made two trips a day, allowing the citizens of Pickens County to visit family, get to work, and shop for necessities. Some people simply rode the train for the sheer pleasure and beautiful scenery enjoyed by a day trip through the foothills. (Photograph courtesy of Dub Fortner.)

BREAK TIME. Although no one is sure of the identity of the people in the photograph, these six African American men are thought to be either workers for the railroad or working for people doing business or traveling on the train. They are resting on a pushcart, a popular tool of the railroad in the late 1800s and early 1900s. (Photograph courtesy of Dub Fortner.)

HUSTLE AND BUSTLE. As in the cover photograph, citizens are gathered outside the depot, including some for traveling, as can be seen by the luggage. Notice the cart parked just under the Easley sign, undoubtedly either picking up or dropping off a load of goods. (Photograph courtesy of Dub Fortner.)

ONE LAST RIDE. This group of children is enjoying a last ride on the Pickens Doodle. With the advent and popularity of the automobile, it became less economically feasible to run the train back and forth to Pickens every day. (Photograph courtesy of the Pickens County Library System.)

FAMILY MEMORY. Those same children pose here with their parents in front of the Doodle. The train was so beloved that its last run became a sort of festival day. Many came from all over to share stories and memories, as well as to say goodbye to the old girl. The Doodle had become such a fixture of the lives of those in town that many were sad to see her go. (Photograph courtesy of the Pickens County Library System.)

16

MAN ON THE TRAIN. The Doodle was special to the citizens of Easley, but it was the major railroad companies that had the larger economic impact. Here an unidentified man poses for a photograph, thought to have been taken in the early 1940s, on one of the larger transport trains that came through town on a regular basis. The logo on the side of the train reads "Southern," indicating that the Atlanta and Charlotte Air Line Company had already been bought out. Along with the new name came an increase in the size and number of trains that came through town. It also allowed for more services to be provided on a more regular basis, such as post services, ice delivery, cotton pick up and drop off, and increased passenger trains. (Photograph courtesy of Dub Fortner.)

R. E. HOLCOMBE FARM. Colonel Holcombe started as a farmer in the area, which provided the basis of his progressive business visions. His farm was sold to the Hester family but is still remembered as the Holcombe farm. Seen here is E. K. Hester baling hay. Although the town did officially begin with the depot, the outlying farms were still considered to be part of Easley and the community as a whole. (Photograph courtesy of Newell Hester.)

MAKING HOUSE CALLS. Dr. Edward F. Wyatt is seen here on his way to a house call. In the late 1800s, there was no official hospital, so doctors traveled through the town and countryside to tend to the patients of Easley. (Photograph courtesy of the Pickens County Library System.)

1915

MOUNT OLIVET CHURCH. Many of the churches in Easley sprouted up to service the needs of the various mill communities, but that was not the case here. Mount Olivet Church was established in 1847 before the town was incorporated. After branching off from Poplar Springs Church, Mount Olivet was a primarily Methodist congregation, although at the time it was considered a "union church"—meaning that it was a house of worship for many denominations. Because of the lack of churches in the area at that time, it was necessary for most of the churches to be union churches. In 1915, an official church building was built in downtown Easley where West View Cemetery is today. It was also used as one of the first schoolhouses. As the congregation grew and the train noise became too intense, the church was relocated to 101 West First Avenue and was renamed the First United Methodist Church. The church has continued to grow and is still one of the main houses of worship in Easley. (Photograph courtesy of the Pickens County Library System.)

PARROTS SERVICE STATION. Fletcher Smith stands alongside his pumps at the Parrot Service Station on Main Street. At that time, in the late 1930s, the station was located across the tracks from the depot and is now a city parking lot for Joe's Ice Cream and other area businesses. (Photograph courtesy of JoAnne Fox.)

THE OTHER SIDE OF THE TRACKS. This view, from the early 1900s, could be confusing to those unfamiliar with the duality of Easley's Main Street as it straddles the railroad. To the left, one can see the depot. On the right is the intersection of Pendleton and Main Streets and many of the commercial buildings that are still in use today. (Photograph courtesy of the Pickens County Library System.)

ROBINSON'S DEPARTMENT STORE. The quintessential department store, Robinson's, established in 1908 by W. W. Robinson, offered everything from the latest fashions to funeral services. The first floor held the store, while embalming and funeral preparation took place on the second floor. The Robinson family moved the funeral services to a separate building on the next block, and both establishments are still in operation today. Pictured are Cleo Bowling (left) and T. M. Jones. (Photograph courtesy of the Pickens County Library System.)

OLD MARKET SQUARE. The square, completed in 1976, was built behind the row of buildings on Main Street to provide parking and a center for civic activities and festivals. The Fourth of July Celebration during the year of the country's bicentennial was the first festival to be held there. (Photograph by B. Owens.)

DOODLE DERAILED. Although the rail was instrumental in the birth and development of Easley, nothing that valuable comes without some complications. On its inaugural trip from Pickens to Easley, it is rumored that the Pickens Doodle derailed. As far as anyone knows, there were no major injuries, and the Doodle quickly became a main source of transportation between the two towns. (Photograph courtesy of Dub Fortner.)

MAN AT BUS STOP. Charlie Welborn poses at a bus stop beside the railroad in 1929. Behind him is a view of West Main Street. To his left, one can see the unique roofline of the Mountain View Hotel, and to the right is a glimpse of the depot. (Photograph courtesy of the Pickens County Library System.)

MOUNTAIN VIEW HOTEL. This 1907 photograph shows one of the first hotels in Easley, the Mountain View. It not only lived up to its name, but was conveniently located on West Main Street a few feet from the depot. (Photograph courtesy of the Pickens County Library System.)

EASLEY BOOKMOBILE. Before the Pickens County Library System built a library in Easley, the Women's Guild of Easley encouraged the citizens to donate used books and money or to volunteer to form a mobile library. Eva Higgins, a prominent and highly civically active citizen of Easley, was instrumental in the operation of the bookmobile. She is pictured above with several local children in 1956. Due to her continued efforts, the vehicle was donated by J. Roper. Higgins is pictured below in the new vehicle with empty shelves waiting to be filled. (Photographs courtesy of the Pickens County Library System.)

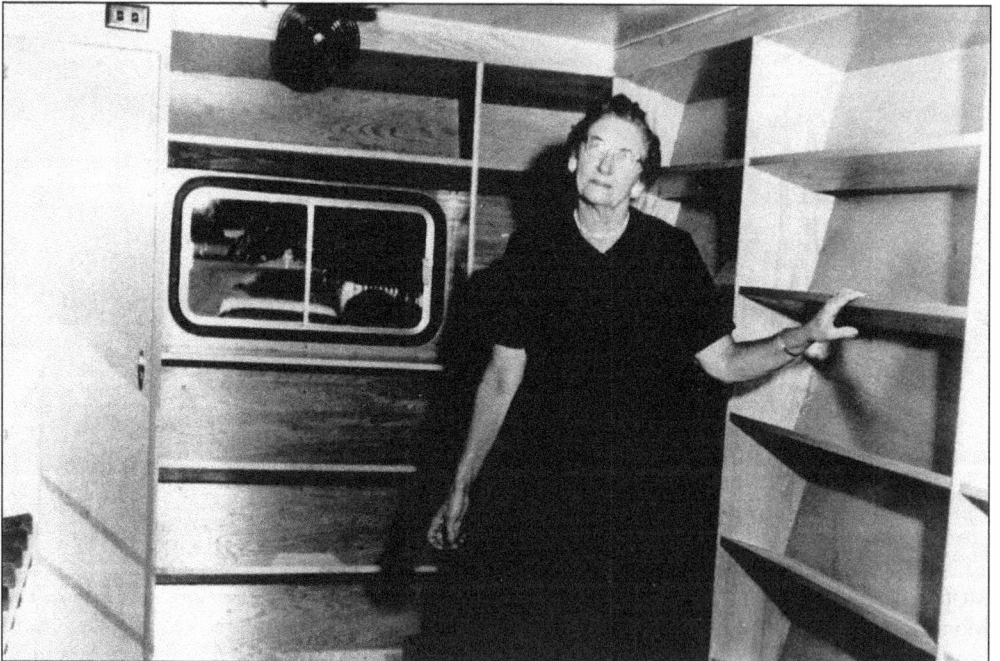

THE POST OFFICE. This small desk was the early post office on Pendleton Street for many years. Easley's post circulated from this desk until an official post office building was granted by the federal government. (Photograph courtesy of Newell Hester.)

THE POST OFFICE. Although there had always been a local postman and a station at the depot for the delivery and pick up of mail, as well as a telegraph office, the town of Easley was not granted an official post office building until 1939. Many of the town's citizens, including the Easley Business Association (later to become the Greater Easley Chamber of Commerce) had petitioned the government for a post office for many years. The first post office was located along the tracks on Main Street. (Photograph courtesy of the Pickens County Library System.)

WEST VIEW CEMETERY. The cemetery was built on the former site of the Mount Olivet Methodist Church. Like everything else downtown, it was built and expanded along the railroad. From this perspective in 1972, one can see Main Street and West Main Street, as well as the tracks running down the middle. (Photograph courtesy of Newell Hester.)

WEST MAIN STREET. In contrast to the picture above, this photograph shows West Main Street in 1936 looking toward the depot and away from the West View Cemetery. Although the years have changed some of the landscape of the downtown area, much remains the same. Most of the original brick storefronts remain, as well as the dual structure of Main Street. (Photograph courtesy of the Pickens County Library System.)

City Hall, Easley, S. C.

May 11, 1922

EARLY CITY HALL. This postcard photograph shows one of the earliest incarnations of the Easley City Hall, complete with stable-type openings for horse-drawn fire wagons. The lack of buildings surrounding this structure indicates that this may even be the first city hall built in Easley. (Photograph courtesy of Dub Fortner.)

J. B. HESTER. Hester was extremely civic minded and was the eighth mayor of Easley, but as seen in this photograph, he did not stray far from his family's roots as farmers and country folk. Pictured shortly after he was out of office, Hester enjoys a ride in his horse-drawn carriage near his family farm. (Photograph courtesy of Newell Hester.)

J. B. Hester

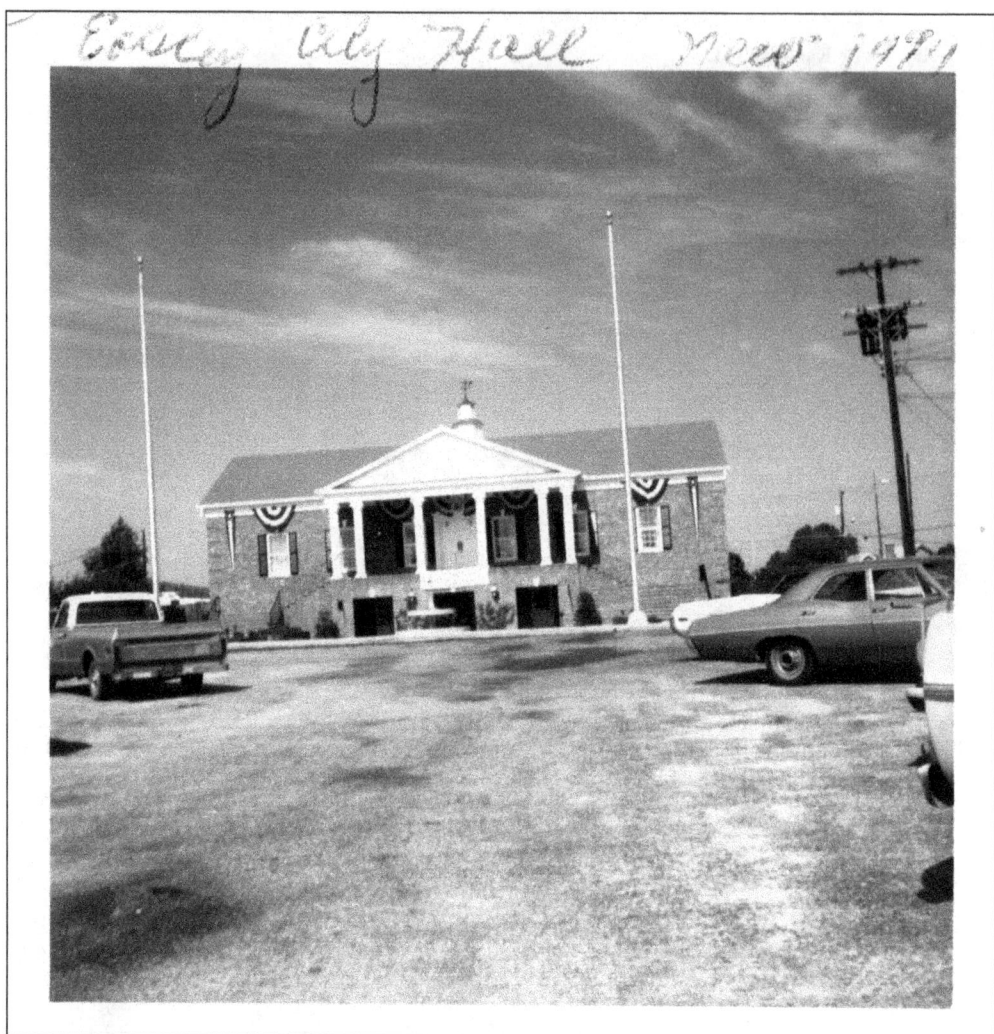

EASLEY CITY HALL. This building is the same city hall that is used today. Located on West Main Street between the West View Cemetery and what is now Mountain View Hotel Antiques, this structure has been rebuilt due to fire and has been renovated several times. The openings at the base of the building were the entrances to the city jail when this picture was taken in 1976. As the city grew, so did the city government, and the space now holds the offices of various departments. Also note the decorations for the country's bicentennial. (Photograph courtesy of Newell Hester.)

WEARING MANY HATS. S. G. Smith, a police officer, stands with man's best friend in several inches of snow, surveying the downtown area. Besides police and fire services, which were established in 1890, the first police chief was also the town lamplighter and trash hauler—in effect a one-man city staff. (Photograph courtesy of the Pickens County Library System.)

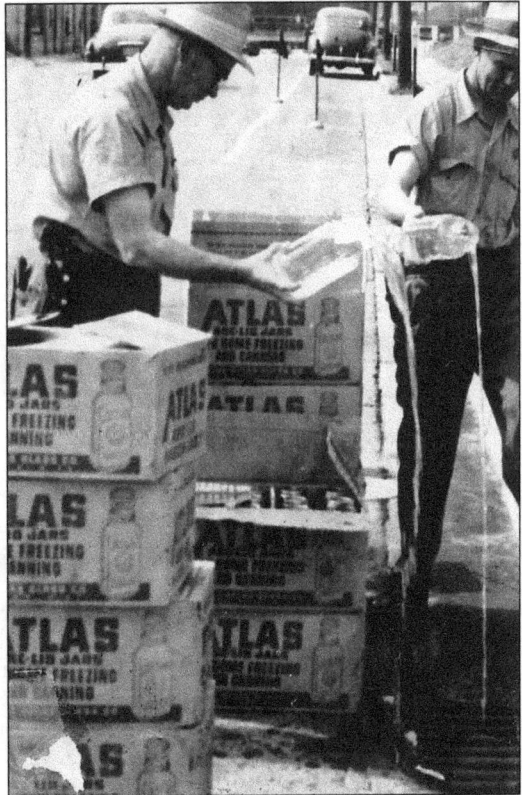

CONTRABAND. City of Easley police officers pour bootleg whiskey into the street drain on West Main Street in front of city hall. The fire department and the police department, along with the offices of the mayor and city council, were housed in the city hall. This scene is a familiar one throughout the South, as running bootleg liquor is often said to be the roots of NASCAR. (Photograph courtesy of Dub Fortner.)

HORSE-DRAWN HEARSE. Although not technically a city service, Robinson's Funeral Home has provided funereal services to the town before some city services were offered. W. W. Robinson originally established both a department store and funeral home in the same building. A ramp led from the second floor, which housed the funeral service area, to the street, where this horse-drawn hearse waited. The Robinson family has preserved this bit of history, and it is still in working order to this day. (Photograph courtesy of Newell Hester.)

SMITH DRUGS. The interior of Smith Drugs in the early 1900s included a soda fountain, and as was common at that time, many of the medications were made on-site by the careful mixing of compounds, as directed by the prescription. Note the long, narrow architecture common to the downtown business district. Most of the original buildings that faced either side of the railroad downtown were designed the same way. (Photograph courtesy of the Pickens County Library System.)

DOWNTOWN FIRE. One of most well-remembered disasters in Easley's history took place on April 25, 1951. Threatening nearly half of the structures on Main Street, Robinson's department store was almost gutted by fire as much of the town looked on. The hearty structure of the brick buildings, many of which had been built in and around the 1880s, and the quick response of the fire department saved the popular store. (Photograph courtesy of Dub Fortner.)

EASLEY FIRE DEPARTMENT. Along with the population boom following World War II, Easley saw a marked growth of economic prosperity in the 1950s and 1960s, causing not only the demand for, but also the capability of increased city services. The 1964 fire department boasted four engines from almost antique to newly acquired, as well as an emergency service vehicle. (Photograph courtesy of Dub Fortner.)

AN AERIAL VIEW OF DOWNTOWN EASLEY. Taken in 1957, this photograph almost completely encapsulates the heart of Easley. This picture makes clear how with one railroad, a town was born. The depot is clearly seen on the left side of the shot along the railroad, and to the right is the distinctive roofline of the Mountain View Hotel. On the other side of the tracks, the intersection of Main Street and Pendleton Street is almost in the center of the photograph. Both streets are lined largely with the original brick buildings that made up the business district. In the upper left corner is the original high school building, which by that time was being used as a sewing plant. (Photograph courtesy of Cam Surrett.)

THE EASLEY ACADEMY. Easley's first official school building was established in 1884. The Academy, as it was called, began its term in January and ran for six months. The first principal was C. W. Moore. (Photograph courtesy of the Pickens County Library System.)

ORIGINAL EASLEY HIGH SCHOOL. The first official Easley High School was located on the corner of First Avenue and Bradley Street in the downtown area. The first class graduated in 1931. (Photograph courtesy of Newell Hester.)

HIGH SCHOOL GYMNASIUM. Located beside the high school, the first Easley High School gymnasium was constructed of wood. To the left of the building, one can see the rear of one of the stores that faced Main Street. (Photograph courtesy of the Pickens County Library System.)

GETTY'S MIDDLE SCHOOL. Formerly Easley Junior High School, Getty's Middle School is the only middle school in Easley. It serves all the children of Easley for grades six through eight. (Photograph by B. Owens.)

DR. ED WYATT. Dr. Wyatt, then just 20 years old, posed with a group of his students. Although no one can properly identify the school, it is logical to think that they could be posing outside the Easley Academy, one of the first school buildings in the area. (Photograph courtesy of the Pickens County Library System.)

LENHARDT SCHOOL HOUSE. According to the Hester family, the Lenhardt School, built in the late 1800s, was the first one-room schoolhouse in Easley. (Photograph courtesy of Newell Hester.)

BRIGHTS STATION SCHOOL. The Brights Station School was located off Lenhardt Road and was used from approximately 1920 until sometime in the 1940s. A small, wooden, two-room structure, the school served the African American children of all ages that lived in the area. (Photograph courtesy of the Pickens County Library System.)

CROSSWELL ELEMENTARY SCHOOL. The first Crosswell School was organized in 1889, when John Easley donated his cotton house for the first school building, with his sister, Carrie Easley, becoming the first teacher. The first year, there were five or six children enrolled. Between 1890 and 1915, the school was rebuilt three times and was relocated to its current location at the intersection of Saluda Dam Road and Kay Drive. The final major renovation converted the school into a brick building in 1980. (Photograph courtesy of the Pickens County Library System.)

CLEARVIEW HIGH SCHOOL. Clearview High, which later became the Simpson Academy, was built to accommodate the African American students in Easley during segregation. Above are the Clearview High Rockets basketball team and cheerleaders in the late 1950s. (Photograph courtesy of the Pickens County Library System.)

THE ARMORY. Citizens of Easley were especially excited when the building of an armory became a reality. As Easley was growing, the new building symbolized the progressive steps that the city was taking. After it was disbanded as an armory, the City of Easley purchased the building, turning it into a city recreational facility in the downtown area. (Photograph courtesy of Newell Hester.)

Two

THE MILL HILL

If this region were a piece of the fabric produced by local textile mills, each strand would contribute its unique quality to a cloth of strength, beauty, and durability . . . a complex, living tapestry of the South Carolina experience: a deftly woven fabric of mountains, mills, and memories.

—South Carolina Department of Parks, Recreation, and Tourism

BOWEN'S CORN MILL. Col. Robert E. Bowen (1830–1909), a Confederate officer, state representative, state senator, and Pickens County businessman, built the gristmill about 1880. Bowen, sensing the future of the milling industry, added a cotton gin soon after construction. (Photograph courtesy of Newell Hester.)

ROADSIDE MARKER. As seen in the accompanying photograph, the mill is no longer in use but is featured among other local historical sites. The South Carolina historical marker stands today. (Photograph by B. Owens.)

GOLDEN CREEK MILL. Built in 1825 by Joseph Woodall in the area that would eventually become Easley, this building was established as a gristmill that provided cornmeal, grits, and flour. Surviving the Civil War, the mill on Golden Creek operated for more than 110 years. Later John Arial added a cotton gin and cotton press, adapting the mill to accommodate the need for textiles and further establishing the textile industry's foothold in the area. In 1985, Joyce and Leroy Stewart purchased land adjacent to the original mill site and, using some parts of the old mill, period pieces, and replicas of the era, rebuilt the mill that stands today. Golden Greek Mill is an official site along the South Carolina National Heritage Corridor. (Photograph by B. Owens.)

Easley oil mill Earley 1900

EASLEY OIL MILL. This was the first industrial mill, and it was the first corporation in the city of Easley. It was established in 1884 as a mechanized agricultural mill that demonstrated the continued industrial growth in the nation as well as in the town. A step beyond the gristmills of the past, the Easley Oil Mill incorporated a cotton gin and press within the first few years of operation. This, of course, paved the way for the burgeoning textile mill industry that would quickly rise in Easley and across the South. Hugh Hamilton added silos sometime in the 1950s. (Photograph courtesy of Newell Hester.)

EASLEY COTTON MILL (PLANT NO. 1) **37,744 SPINDLES—1020 LOOMS.** EASLEY, S. C.

EASLEY COTTON MILL. In 1899, John Greer convinced the citizens of Easley to organize a capital stock of $200,000 to bring the Easley Cotton Mill into town, as opposed to farming and shipping cotton to neighboring communities. It was the first cotton mill in Easley. Greer served as the first president. At its beginning, the mill built 50 homes for its employees; however, by the 1940s, there were at least 300 homes, as well as a company store, churches, and schools. (Photograph courtesy of Dub Fortner.)

GLENWOOD MILLS
DIVISION OF
MAYFAIR MILLS
EASLEY, SOUTH CAROLINA

GLENWOOD COTTON MILL. This mill was the second mill built in Easley. It was chartered on February 6, 1902. W. M. Hagood Sr. was instrumental in the birth of the mill and was elected president. The Hagood family contributed to the growth of the textile industry and the town at large. The Glenwood mill also fostered its own community, complete with a company store, hundreds of homes, two churches, and a school. (Photograph courtesy of Dub Fortner.)

E MANUFACTURING CO. (COTTON MILL) 36,764 SPINDLES, 948 LOOMS.   EASLEY, S. C

ALICE MILL. E. H. Shanklin founded the Alice Mill in 1910 with the capital stock of $200,000. He was also the first president. As the mill grew in size, the village surrounding the mill provided more homes and services for its workers. In the 1920s, the mill was purchased by the McKissick family. They then went on to create four more large mills in Easley under the name of the Alice Manufacturing Company. (Photograph courtesy of the Owens family.)

CARDING ROOM. Unidentified employees bustle through their workday at the Alice Mill in the 1950s. (Photograph courtesy of Dub Fortner.)

"LOONIES." Coins or sometimes tickets were issued by each mill for certain amounts. This served multiples purposes. In some cases, the employees could get an advance or loan from the mill, but it was issued in "loonies," ensuring that the money could only be spent at the company store. In some ways it was a form of a credit system, but it seemingly indebted the employee to the store to an undue amount. These loonies are collectables today, and the system of the loonies and the company store has even been immortalized in song: "I owe my soul to the company store." (Photograph courtesy of Tony Chibbaro.)

ARIAL PLANT. As the Alice Manufacturing Company grew, a second plant was built. The mill was built on a hill that bore the name of Airialles, a family of French descent that had owned the land. The hill, plant, and village that grew up around it bear the Americanized spelling of Arial. (Photograph courtesy of Dub Fortner.)

CENSUS OF EASLEY. In 1916, the three large cotton mills were the Glenwood, Easley, and Alice mills. With a population of just 3,744, a vast majority of the town was in some way employed or housed by the three major mills. (Photograph courtesy of Dub Fortner.)

Census of Easley

Taken Nov. 1, 1916, by L. B. O'Dell.

WHITES.		COLORED.	
Number Males - - -	678	Number of Males - - -	211
Number Females - - -	621	Number of Females - - -	203
Number of Boys - - -	820	Number of Boys - - -	218
Number of Girls - - -	788	Number of Girls - - -	215
Total White Population	2897	Total Colored Population	847

Total Population of the City of Easley, 3744.

EASLEY HAS:

Seventy-Five Business Houses, Three Large Cotton Mills, One Oil Mill and Fertilizer Mfg. Co., Two Ginneries, One Flour Mills, Two Grist Mills, Two Banks, One Building and Loan Association, Two Hotels, Eleven White Churches, all full on Sundays; Three Colored Churches, Four White Graded Schools with a total attendance of 849; One Colored Graded School, One Electric Power and Water Plant, Two Dentists, One Studio, One Lawyer, Five Physicians, Five Restaurants, One Brass Band, Electric Lights, Water Works·

GLENWOOD WATER TOWER. As the Glenwood mill village was being built and expanded, mill employees constructed the water tower in 1905 to supply the entire village. The mill communities were self-sufficient in many ways, and in this case they had to be, as there was no citywide water system. (Photograph courtesy of Dub Fortner.)

MILL EMPLOYEES. Glenwood mill employees pose for a group photograph. This was a common practice among all the mills throughout the years. In this case, the group is the first shift at the Glenwood mill in October 1955. (Photograph courtesy of Dub Fortner.)

INSIDE THE MILL. An unidentified woman works in the spooling room at an Easley Cotton Mill in the early 1950s. (Photograph courtesy of Dub Fortner.)

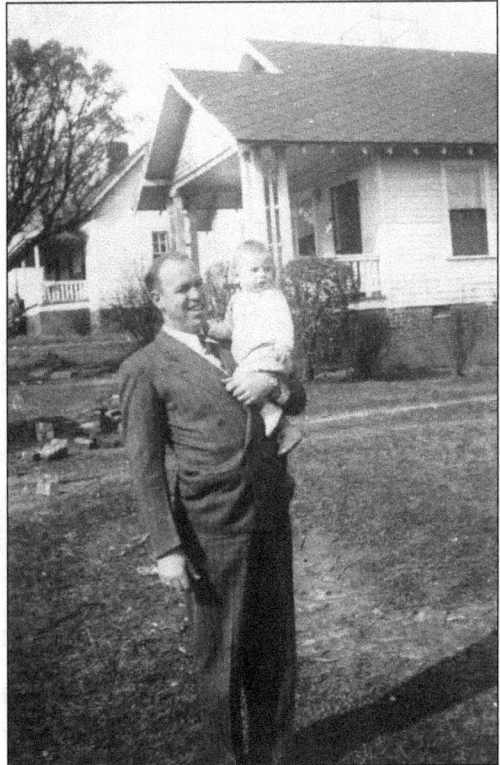

J. B. "RED" OWENS AND SON, JOHN OWENS. This perspective of Sixth Street, part of an Easley Cotton Mill village, shows an average mill house and the row structure of the houses in the neighborhood. The Owenses stand in their yard. Aunts, uncles, and cousins occupied most of the surrounding homes, as was common within each mill village. (Photograph courtesy of the Owens family.)

DURING THE WAR. The Easley mills were forced to rely on the female population to supplement the workforce of the mills during World War II because so many young men went off to war. From left to right are Nell Hood, Irving Hood, Mrs. Charles Ballew, Charles Ballew and Andrew Ballew. (Photograph courtesy of Dub Fortner.)

HOUSES ON GARRISON STREET. This closer view of the distinctive bungalow style of homes that line the mill hills makes it a bit clearer how similar all the houses on the hill were. Not that it mattered to the families that lived there, as most folks who grew up on the hill treated their neighbors as family, and the children treated every yard as their own. (Photograph courtesy of Dub Fortner.)

DON AND CRICK DODGENS. This lovely young couple prepares to start their married lives by moving into a mill bungalow after World War II. Many young men came home to join their families working in the mills. (Photograph courtesy of Dub Fortner.)

THE BENJAMINS. Francis and Olin Benjamin are also beginning their lives as a couple on the mill hill. Behind the two are the Glenwood mill and the water tower that supplied the village and mill. (Photograph courtesy of Dub Fortner.)

W. M. HAGOOD AND COMPANY BILL OF SALE. W. M. Hagood and family are mention throughout this volume as an example of a brilliant business enterprise and progressive entrepreneurs. This bill of sale from the 1880s states that they were dealers in dry goods and other merchandise, but it was the cotton purchasing and distribution that led to one of the first cotton mills in Easley. (Photograph courtesy of the Pickens County Library System.)

BOY ON A PORCH. J. C. Fortner poses almost like an adult on the front porch of his mill home at the beginning of the 20th century. In the heat of the summer, the shade of the porch was the coolest place to rest after work if one could not get to a nearby river or lake. (Photograph courtesy of Dub Fortner.)

LIFE ON THE MILL HILL. Liza Owens poses in front of her family home in the Easley Cotton Mill village. Most mill homes were approximately four rooms, and she shared this particular home with up to six other family members. (Photograph courtesy of Dub Fortner.)

FAMILY AND DOG. The Owens family of the Easley Cotton Mill village is an example of a typical mill hill family. All four members of the family pose in front of their home on Sixth Street in the early 1900s. Lela and Leo Owens sit with their son, Joseph Bennet or "J. B.," and the fourth member of the family, Leo's dog. (Photograph courtesy of the Owens family.)

EARLY EASLEY RESIDENTS. In the early 1900s, a group of unidentified young women pose for a portrait in the great outdoors. This was the easiest way to capture a picture at the time. (Photograph courtesy of Dub Fortner.)

HORSING AROUND. An excited Jerry Owens poses on a pony outside his family home. (Photograph courtesy of Dub Fortner.)

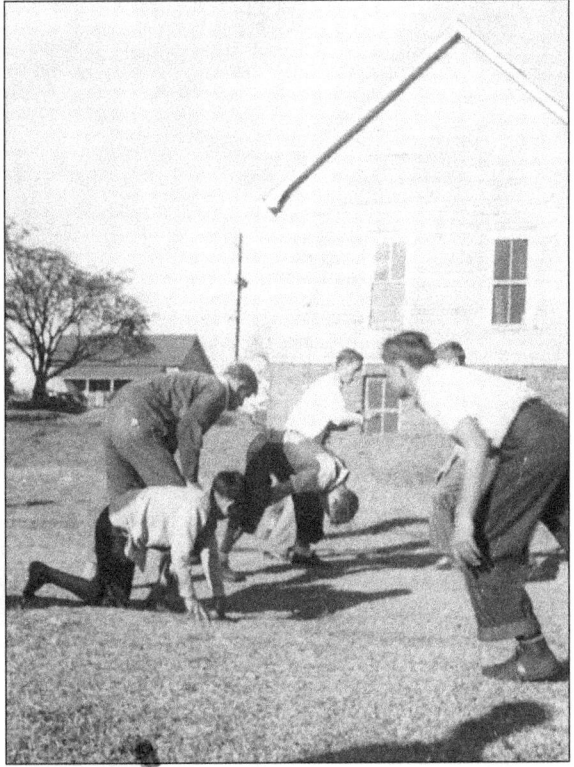

DOWN, SET, HUT! Anyone who grew up on a mill hill can tell you that these two scenes are far from unusual. In a time and culture when it truly did take a village to raise a child, the children of the mill villages went to school together, attended church together, and roamed through each other's yards. It was also common for a mom to bandage a neighborhood child's skinned knee or let his or her parents know when a child had misbehaved. In these photographs, the children are seen playing behind the Glenwood mill company store. (Photographs courtesy of Dub Fortner.)

ARIAL MILL BASEBALL. The mills provided many forms of recreation, from a pool, to tennis, to the most esteemed game—baseball. This team played for the Arial Mill in 1939. (Photograph courtesy of Dub Fortner.)

GLENWOOD BASEBALL. This photograph was taken of a Glenwood mill baseball team in the 1940s. One wonders how the young men pictured above had the energy to play a game after working in the mill all week. (Photograph courtesy of Dub Fortner.)

SLUGGERS. This is the Easley Cotton Mill Sluggers team from the 1930s. From left to right are (first row) Joe Anders, Jesse Henson, Coon Hendricks, Paul Rampey, Earley Bagwell, Carvin Medlock, and unidentified; (second row) Fred Marsh, Harry Ashworth, James Campbell, Hal Ensley, Verlon McIntyre, Juber Harriston, and unidentified. (Photograph courtesy of Dub Fortner.)

REUNION. A group of gentlemen from the various mill baseball teams gathers together for a reunion of players. This is a common occurrence, and in this case, these men are also veterans of World War II. (Photograph courtesy of Dub Fortner.)

EASLEY MILL TEAM. The Easley Cotton Mill had an extensive recreation department for its community, providing tennis courts, a pool, football, and, of course, baseball. Members of the 1949 team are pictured, including Bobby Ponder, Wallace Browning, Bruce Stansell, Bill Fortner, Lawrence Southerland, coach B. B. McKivey, Jack Owens, Bob Rankin, Raymond Jewell, George Owens, and Garvin Hunter. (Photograph courtesy of Dub Fortner.)

ALICE MANUFACTURING COMPANY TEAM. Although the Easley Cotton Mill may have had a more extensive program, the Alice Mill Ball Park has been a staple for baseball fans in Easley for generations. It was home to the mill team and the American Legion Post No. 52 team. The year and the identities of the players in this photograph are unknown. (Photograph courtesy of Dub Fortner.)

GLENWOOD BAPTIST CHURCH. The Glenwood Baptist Church was organized on October 25, 1908, on Hagood Street next to the Glenwood mill. As the mill and church grew, it became necessary to move the church to a brick structure on Saco Lowell Road in 1962. The educational building of the church still stands on the mill site and was used by the mill as an office building. (Photograph courtesy of the Pickens County Library System.)

GLENWOOD WESLEYAN METHODIST CHURCH. First organized in 1907, the church was disbanded in 1909, though no records indicate why. Reorganized in 1920, the congregation used the Glenwood Methodist Church building until land could be purchased and their own church built on Barton Street in 1924. Soon after, the church became simply Glenwood Wesleyan Church, and its final reconstruction moved the church to Hagood Street in 1964, where it is located today. This is a good example of the dedication to their faith of those living in the mill communities. Easley Cotton Mill, Arial Mill, and Alice Mill had several churches of different denominations within blocks of each other and within easy walking distance from the mill homes. (Photograph courtesy of the Pickens County Library System.)

Three

FAMILIES, COMMUNITY, FELLOWSHIP

The American city should be a collection of communities where every member has a right to belong. It should be a place where every man feels safe on his streets and in the house of his friends. It should be a place where each individual's dignity and self-respect is strengthened by the respect and affection of his neighbors. It should be a place where each of us can find the satisfaction and warmth which comes from being a member of the community of man. This is what man sought at the dawn of civilization. It is what we seek today.

—Lyndon B. Johnson

THE BETTER BABY SHOW. Since the dawn of time, mothers have found their babies to be the most beautiful and perfect. Apparently, the same applied for many Easley mothers, who showed off their children at the Pickens County Fair in 1920. (Photograph courtesy of the Pickens County Library System.)

YOUNG MAN IN A CARRIAGE. A youthful Robert Hester poses with his horse and carriage outside his family home. The Hester family, having contributed to the growth of Easley through the mills, schools, and farming, afforded the young man the luxury of his own transportation. (Photograph courtesy of Newell Hester.)

JAMES BENJAMIN HESTER AND FAMILY. Pictured in 1898, the Hester family is, from left to right, (seated) Sallie, J. B., Lucetta, Susie, and Ralph; (standing) W. B., Baylus, Robert, Elliot, and E. G. J. B. Hester, who was the eighth mayor of Easley, from 1883 through 1885. (Photograph courtesy of Newell Hester.)

THE GARRETT HOME. William R. A. Garrett poses with his family outside his home at the corner of B Street and East Main Street. (Photograph courtesy of the Pickens County Library System.)

WALKER HOME. Dr. J. C. Walker and his family enjoyed the benefits that came with being one of few physicians in the area. Along with the luxury of owning ponies and cows, they were also able to remodel their home from one story into this lovely two-story home in downtown Easley between 1900 and 1913. (Photograph courtesy of the Pickens County Library System.)

THE WAR EFFORT. W. M. Hopkins shows his patriotic spirit by setting up a sign and collection site on Main Street, encouraging the citizens of Easley to donate scrap metal to recycle for our boys "over there." (Photograph courtesy of the Pickens County Library System.)

Festival. This fall fair and parade seems to have been attended by almost everyone in Easley and the surrounding area. The train can barely be seen behind all the fairgoers gathered on Main Street. (Photograph courtesy of the Pickens County Library System.)

Election Returns Board. A crowd has gathered outside the T. E. Jones Furniture Company on Pendleton Street to watch the local election results, and judging by the faces of the crowd, the results were also an excuse for folks to get together for fellowship. The display board, sponsored by the *Easley Progress*, kept a running tally of votes as they came in. The board was being kept by Woodrow M. Hopkins on August 27, 1940. (Photograph courtesy of the Pickens County Library System.)

"SHORTY" EARL RUSSELL. Pictured during World War II, the imposing figure of Russell in his uniform hints to the strength and fortitude he would later show, along with his family, with a progressive business and civic vision, contributing to the growth of Easley through the textile industry and active citizenship. (Photograph courtesy of the Pickens County Library System.)

DR. CHARLES TRIPP, ALEC ROBINSON, AND ELLISON MCKISSICK SR. Pictured from left to right are three of the most influential men in various fields—medical, retail, business, and textiles—who are enjoying a beautiful foothills afternoon in the late 1950s. One would hope that they were taking the time to relax, but it is more probable that they were discussing business. (Photograph courtesy of the Pickens County Library System.)

ROBERT PICKENS. At the time of this photograph in the 1930s, Robert Pickens of the Pickens family, for which the county was named, was the oldest living Confederate soldier in Easley. (Photograph courtesy of the Pickens County Library System.)

BUCK'S DRIVE-IN. Buck Surrett (left) and Roy Chapman pose outside the drive-through window of the new drive-in in the early 1960s. It was not long before Buck's became a popular spot for lunch, meetings, and the occasional dignitary visit. (Photograph courtesy of Cam Surrett.)

THE VICE PRESIDENT VISITS. In February 1988, then–U.S. vice president George Bush visited the Upstate area. Stopping for lunch in Easley, he is seen here enjoying a "meat and three" lunch with South Carolina governor Carol Campbell and citizens of Easley at Buck's. (Photograph by the *Greenville News*, provided by Cam Surrett.)

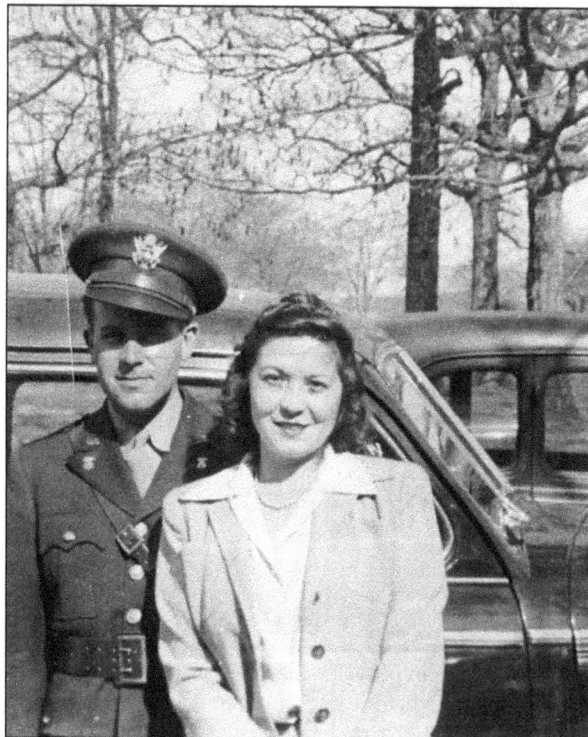

R. CARL BYARS AND FRANCES BYARS. The Byars family settled in Easley when Methodist circuit rider Rev. David Dero Byars moved to the area. His descendant Carl Byars married Frances after World War II. When their children were school-aged, Frances, along with others in the community, polled the area for pregnant women and those with small children, thereby convincing the district to build the East End School. Carl bought the land from a Mr. Wyatt and built the school where it stands today. Because of their accomplishments, Carl received the Order of the Palmetto when he was 90 years old, and Frances received the Order of the Silver Crescent at the age of 90. (Photograph courtesy of the Byars family.)

HERE COMES SANTA CLAUS. Festivals and parades were and continue to be a staple of small-town life and served to bring the community together. Here onlookers greet Santa Claus, the main attraction of the annual Easley Christmas Parade, on Main Street in the early 1970s. (Photograph courtesy of the Pickens County Library System.)

SOUTHERN BELLES. The Southern Belles Women's Club, much like their male counterparts in the Lions Club, was always active in promoting community growth and planning fund-raisers. In this photograph, taken in 1968, the ladies are dressed in costume in preparation for the Pickens County Centennial festivities. (Photograph courtesy of the Pickens County Library System.)

69

MISS EASLEY. Like other towns across the South, Easley has no shortage of beauty queens. What parade would be complete without them, not to mention the civic contributions made by the lovely girls? Miss Easley 1970, Jeannie Whitlock, rides in the Easley Christmas Parade. (Photograph courtesy of the Pickens County Library System.)

HOME OF MINNIE CRENSHAW HENDRICKS. The Hendricks family started as farmers in the area, and through the boom in cotton sales, they were able to acquire vast amounts of property, building wealth that allowed them to invest and support the growth of many city institutions. Among those pictured are May, Eva, Nora, and Elaine Finley, Felix and James Crockett, and in-laws John Anthony and John Fraley. (Photograph courtesy of Lib Oates.)

ELLISON AND JEAN MCKISSICK. The McKissick family is perhaps the most influential family in the textile industry in Easley. A progressive lot, different members have been responsible for the building of the Alice Manufacturing Company (which at one point had five major plants in operation in the area), contributed to churches and schools, and provided untold involvement in multiple civic organizations. (Photograph courtesy of the Pickens County Library System.)

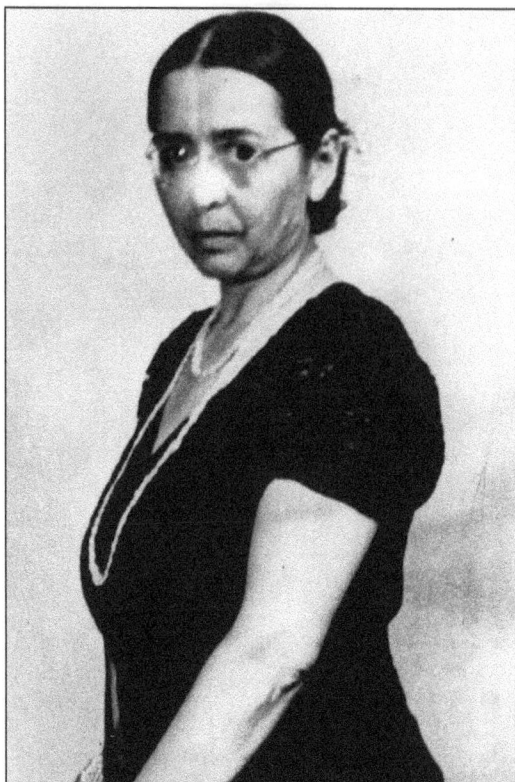

MAY BETH JOHNSON CAMP. One of the most beloved music teachers in the Easley schools, Camp taught hundreds of the children of town through her career of nearly three decades. (Photograph courtesy of the Pickens County Library System.)

EASLEY COMMUNITY BAND. Music has always played an extremely important role in the lives of the citizens of Easley. As early as 1915, the town had a community band. Eventually, the major mills also had their own bands or singing groups, but the original band was truly for the whole community. They performed at festivals, weddings, funerals, and parades. (Photograph courtesy of the Pickens County Library System.)

EASLEY BRASS BAND. Probably the first organized community band in Easley, the gentlemen above posed for this photograph in the early 1900s. Although the exact date is unknown, one can determine from the style of dress the approximate year as well as the varying backgrounds of the men, from farmer to businessman. Among those pictured are John Bowen, J. E. Parsons, B. F. McElreath, Elias Hunter, Samuel Hester, H. E. Russell, P. C. Johnson, R. H. Holcombe, E. Hester, and R. Hester. (Photograph courtesy of Newell Hester.)

THE STRONGEST MAN IN THE COUNTRY. The Easley Football Jamboree, held at Easley Junior High School, has always been a major event for the townsfolk. In the 1960s, Paul Anderson was said to be the strongest man in the country. He had appeared on various television shows, and while in Easley, he not only lifted a dozen women seated on a table, but he also pounded a nail through a board with his bare hand. It was quite a show, and they had not even gotten to the football game yet! (Photograph courtesy of Dub Fortner.)

EASLEY LIONS CLUB. Of all the ways for serious, community-minded men to draw attention and raise funds for their civic organizations' causes, one of the most amusing and effective is the womanless pageant or womanless wedding. It takes a brave and determined business owner, mill worker, or farmer to dress in drag for something he believes in. (Photograph courtesy of Dub Fortner.)

THE *EASLEY PROGRESS*. In 1902, a group of Easley businessmen formed Easley Publications. Maj. David F. Bradley, the original publisher, composed an introductory editorial that appeared in that first issue of the *Progress*, in which he promised the newspaper would cover the news as it happened and would always be "a welcome visitor in your home." The weekly paper has served the citizens of Easley for more than 106 years. (Photograph by B. Owens.)

J. H. Orr, — PHOTOGRAPHER, — Elberton, Ga.

AUGUSTA AMELIA BARTON HIGGINS. As the town grew, farmland turned into neighborhoods and part of the inner city. In naming the streets and schools, often the family name associated with the land was honored. Augusta Higgins was one of the oldest citizens in town when the road was constructed on land that had been part of the Higgins farm. She and many other members of her family were active in the community and were highly esteemed. This photograph was donated with great pride by her granddaughter, Augusta Elizabeth Higgins Oates, who was also named after this amazing woman. (Photograph courtesy of Lib Oates.)

WILLIAM H. HAGOOD HOME 1909. The Hagoods were an extremely influential family in the growth of the city of Easley. Beginning with the farming and sales of cotton to other mills in the area, William Hagood was instrumental in bringing textile mills into Easley. Seen above is the family homestead, and judging by its size, one can assume the cotton and textile manufacturing industries were lucrative for the Hagoods. The family is also known for its civic involvement and commitment to its community. (Photograph courtesy of Newell Hester.)

J. B. HESTER BIRTHPLACE. Many great men and women come from humble beginnings. J. B. Hester was a progressive member of the community, a businessman, and mayor. This small clapboard dwelling in which he was born would have fit into one room of his large family home in the downtown area, also pictured in this volume. (Photograph courtesy of Newell Hester.)

DR. LLEWELLYN CALHOUN JOHNSON. A rare site in the early 1920s, Dr. Johnson was one of the first female physicians in the Upstate. Her office was located on Main Street. A well-respected member of the community, she is an example of the many strong women who contributed to the growth of Easley. (Photograph courtesy of the Pickens County Library System.)

THE GREATER EASLEY CHAMBER OF COMMERCE. In the early 1930s, a group of businessmen gathered together to create the Easley Business Association in order to further the economic growth of the town through cooperation, suggested legislation, and community programs. The goal was to draw attention to the commercial possibilities as well as the civic duty of the businesses established. The group informally disbanded during World War II, only to become an officially chartered chamber of commerce in 1947 under the watchful eye of Jack Ragsdale, among many others. (Photograph courtesy of the Greater Easley Chamber of Commerce.)

MASONIC TEMPLE. Located in the downtown area, Bates Lodge No. 189 is the local chapter of the Ancient Order of Freemasons. The fraternal organization had existed in the area for many years, with many of the founding fathers of Easley being members, including R. E. Holcombe and Gen. William King Easley. However, the Bates Lodge did not occupy its current home until 1942. The building was originally the Easley First Baptist Church. The Bates Lodge has always played a large role in the community, raising funds for multiple charities, participating in most city events, and serving as a networking and supportive society for many prominent citizens. (Photograph courtesy of the Pickens County Library System.)

"LAF-O-RAMA." As has always been true in Easley, the community loves a chance to come together, usually to sing, laugh, and talk. In this case, a talent show was held in the Easley High School Auditorium in 1960. There were clowns, comedians, singers, and, obviously, dancers. (Photograph courtesy of the Pickens County Library System.)

BRIGGS AND ARNOLD HOME. This house (pictured above) is the birthplace of Eliza Caroline Arnold, the wife of R. E. Holcombe. The Briggs family was also related by marriage to the Hester family, a civic-minded family mentioned several times in this volume. (Photograph courtesy of Newell Hester.)

MISS SOUTH CAROLINA. In 1973, Fran Jean Riggins was crowned the first Miss South Carolina from Easley. She was 21 years old at the time and attended Clemson University. (Photograph courtesy of the Riggins family.)

PALMETTO STOCK FARM. When thinking about the community of Easley, one cannot forget the many farms that skirted the heart of town. The Palmetto Stock Farm was a successful farm in Easley owned by T. B. Higgins. This photograph illustrates the amount of man power and hard work that went into running a successful farm. Two generations of the Higgins family, including Augusta Elizabeth Higgins, worked and lived on the land that would one day be swallowed up by the town. The family's contribution to the town has never been forgotten. (Photograph courtesy of Lib Oates.)

FORTNER PHOTO ALBUM. It is unclear if this is a page from strictly a family photo album or an album of a collection of friends. In any case, the page itself is a beautiful example of portrait photography from the era. From left to right are (first row), Peggy Stansell, unidentified, Sarah Chapman, Faye Couch, and Grace Coker; (second row) Annie Hughes, Kathleen Fortner, Mae Campbell, Lloyd and Pauline Bryant, and Lynell Rankin; (third row) Hattie Knox, Lena Huff, Melanie Weaver, Jamie Woods, and unidentified; (fourth row) Leila C. Fortner, Roy Hester, Edna Hester, Helen R. Adcox, and Agnes Hopkins. (Photograph courtesy of Dub Fortner.)

EASLEY HIGH SCHOOL BAND. Not only have celebrities visited our small town, but Easley has also produced a few celebrities of its own. This ensemble from 1954 appeared on *The Bob Poole Show*. From left to right are (first row) Martha Rankin, Leon Ballentine, Mary Carpenter, Edwinn McCravey, Bernice Williams Tribble, Ralph Hendricks, Jack Taylor, Larry James, and Larry Brown; (second row) Joanne Smith Fox, Donnie Tribble, Oliver Christopher, and Foster Gentry. (Photograph courtesy of Jo Anne Fox.)

CITY COUNCIL AND GUESTS. During that 1970s, the Easley City Council was honored by the presence of government dignitaries. Pictured from left to right are Mayor C. Ellenburg, Congressman Bryan Dorn, Councilman J. B. Owens, Gen. William Westmoreland, Sandy Hagood, Joe Young, Earl Morris, and Mrs. Earl Morris. During the same time, Lyndon B Johnson also visited Easley, having lunch with several civic organizations, council members, and citizens at Buck's Drive In. (Photograph courtesy of the Owens family.)

WILLIAM SCOTT. Scott was the superintendent of schools for several decades. He poses here on horseback while performing in a horse show in the early 1960s. (Photograph courtesy of the Pickens County Library System.)

JOHN A. ROPER. An entrepreneur and civic leader, Roper began the Easley Bank and the Roper Motor Company. Known for his hands-on approach and friendly attitude toward his employees and customers, Roper was well respected in the community. (Photograph courtesy of Angie Sheriff.)

MR. AND MRS. J. A. ROPER. Shown here with his wife, John Roper stayed active in his businesses well into his 90s. Celebrating his 90th birthday at the Roper Motor Company, he is affectionately referred to as "The Boss" on the cake. His bank and dealership were two of the longest running operations in Easley's history. (Photograph courtesy of Angie Sherriff.)

MUSIC IN EASLEY. From the city's band, to the individual mill bands, to various family ensembles—the Owens Quartet, for example—groups provided music for all types of gatherings and often just for fun. Pictured is the Higgins family band. From left to right are Sirrine Higgins, Victor Higgins, A. K. Higgins, and Jim Higgins; in back is Byron Higgins. (Photograph courtesy of Lib Oates.)

THE COTTON PICKERS. This semi-professional basketball team dominated their league between 1954 and 1964. In those five years, the team lost only 7 games and won 193. From left to right are (seated) managers Roosevelt Robinson and Spencer Collins; (standing) Shine Wels, Johnny White, Pete Ladd, Benny Adams, Phil Williams, Jon Hodge, and unidentified. (Photograph courtesy of Dub Fortner.)

AMERICAN LEGION. Easley's American Legion Post No. 52 baseball team poses in 1949 at the Alice Mill baseball field, their home field, while a few unidentified fans observe. From left to right are (kneeling) Bobby Rankin, Ronnie Bryant, John Seaborn, Paul Chastain, Charles Smith, and Leland Pilgrim; (standing) Sonny Lollis, Walter Wiggins, Donnie Garrison, Cotton Creek, J. M. Ellison, Jerry Wilson, and Rudy Evatt. (Photograph courtesy of Dub Fortner.)

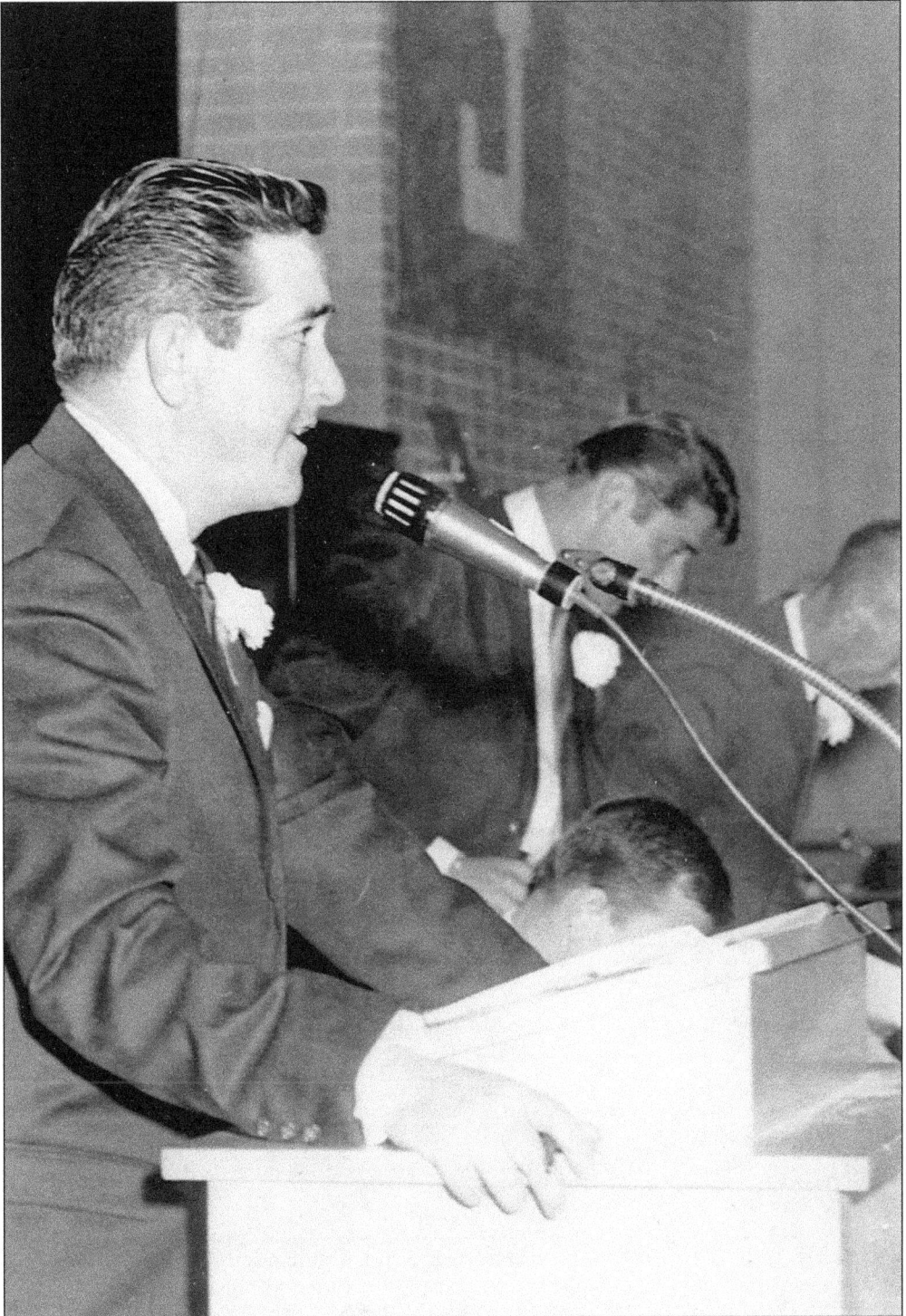

Big Name. At the Easley Football Jamboree in the late 1960s, coach Bill Carr introduces professional football player and hall of famer Joe Namath. Namath spoke to a packed house at the Easley Junior High auditorium. (Photograph courtesy of Cam Surrett.)

STROM THURMOND AT WOODSIDE. In 1949, then–South Carolina governor Strom Thurmond (center), perhaps one of the most notable senators in the history of the U.S. Congress, visited the Woodside Ball Park for this photo opportunity with Easley native and Woodside Mill team manager Joe Anders (right) and former Detroit Tiger pitcher Floyd Geibel (left). (Photograph courtesy of Dub Fortner.)

MARIE AND EARL JAMES MAY. The Mays pose here with Jim McConnell's steam engine, which was on display for Easley's celebration of the U.S. Bicentennial in 1976. The steam engine was not only reminiscent of the country's youth, but was also especially symbolic for the town of Easley because it began with a steam engine on a rail. (Photograph courtesy of Marie May.)

BICENTENNIAL PARADE. Unidentified men ride atop an old-fashioned fire pump in the 1976 bicentennial parade down Main Street. The parade was a special one for Easley. The town was extremely prosperous, and although the depot had been torn down a few years earlier, the textile industry, along with the town's population and economy, was booming. (Photograph courtesy of Marie May.)

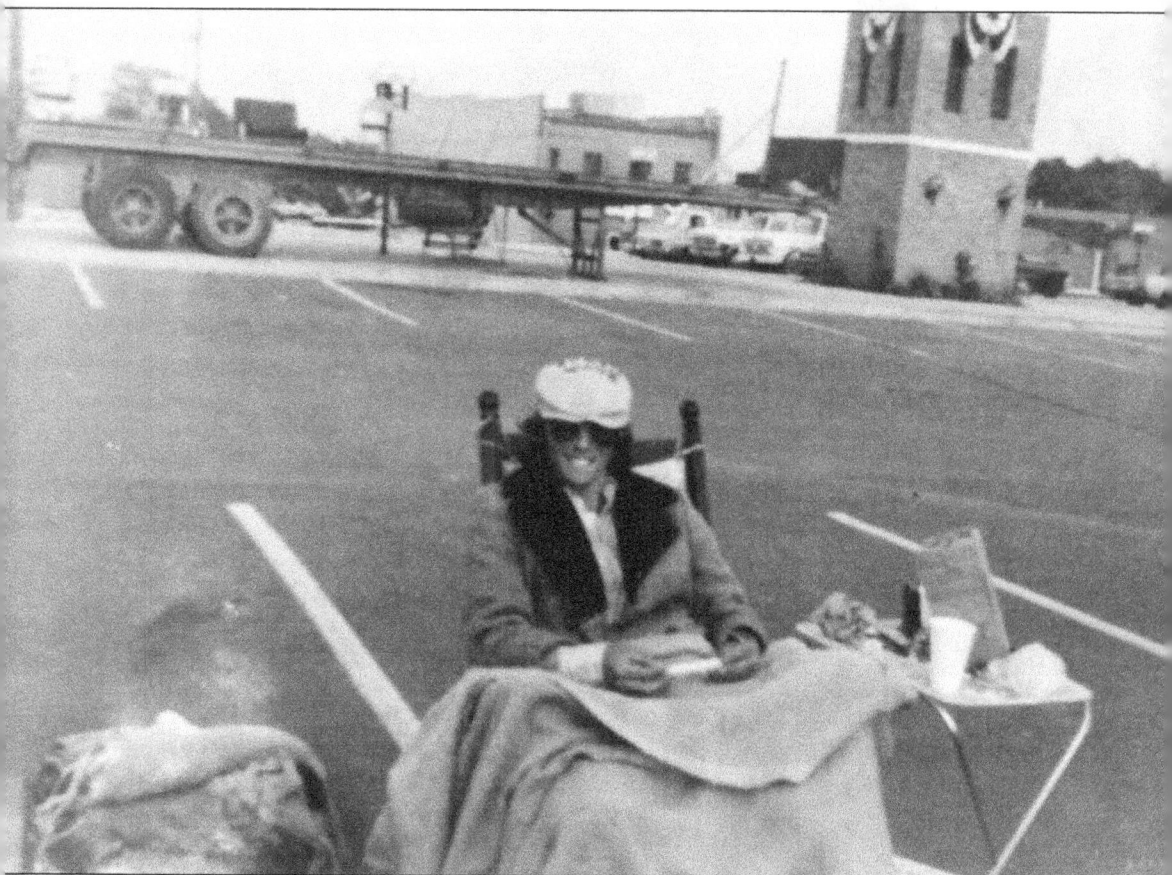

JIMMY MAY. An example of Easley's prosperity was the completion of the Old Market Square, which conveniently coincided with the celebration of the Fourth of July in 1976. Jimmy May participates in a rocking chair marathon held in the newly finished square in which the contestants competed to see who could remain in the chair and in motion, leaving only for short bathroom breaks. (Photograph courtesy of Marie May.)

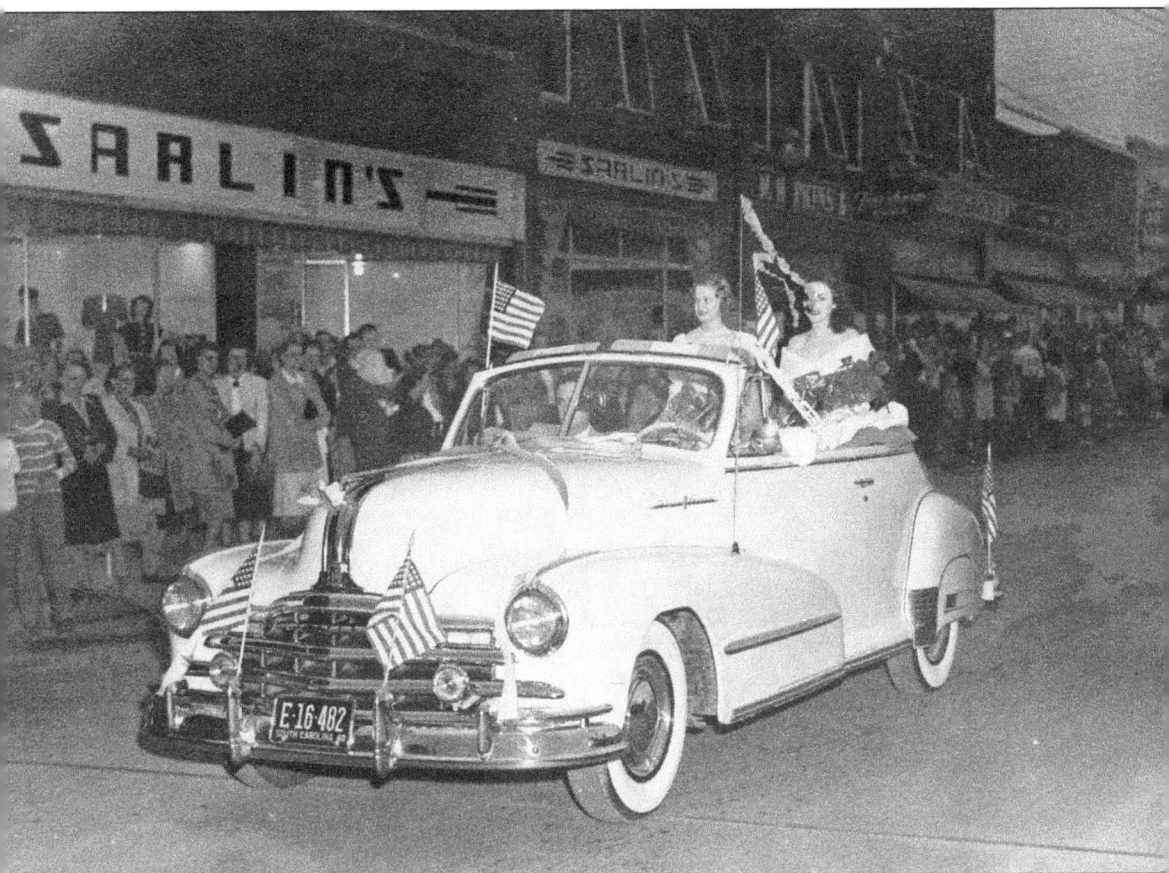

Spring Festival. Every season and holiday is reason to celebrate in Easley. These celebrations keep the community close and give friends and family a chance to catch up. At this spring festival on May 6, 1948, drivers George Green (left) and Dub Fortner chauffeur beauty queens Martha Ann Reeves (left) and JoAnne Powell. (Photograph courtesy of Dub Fortner.)

FIRST UNITED METHODIST CHURCH. The First United Methodist, located at 101 West First Avenue, is the current incarnation of the first church established in Easley—Mount Olivet Church. Transplanted from Main Street due to the need for a larger facility and to avoid some of the noise caused by the train, the current building was constructed in 1930 and has undergone renovations throughout the years. (Photograph courtesy of the Pickens County Library System.)

A CONGREGATION. Pictured in 1940 is the congregation of Easley First Baptist Church at its original location on Main Street. (Photograph courtesy of the Pickens County Library System.)

FIRST BAPTIST CHURCH AND REV. D. W. HIOTT. Established in 1875, the original building was constructed at the corner of Main Street and North B Street, where it stood for 34 years. Also shown is the church's first pastor, Rev. David Weston Hiott Sr. After the original wood building was destroyed by fire in 1917, a brick building was constructed in its place, which would later become the Masonic temple. The church moved to its present location in 1952. (Photograph courtesy of the Pickens County Library System.)

CROSSROADS BAPTIST CHURCH. This large group of children poses outside Crossroads Baptist Church to commemorate the first Bible school commencement in 1947. The church had been organized in 1814, but the land was not purchased until August 1875. The church still occupies the same land, although the building has been through several renovations. At one time, the nearby Doddy's Creek was used for baptisms. (Photograph courtesy of the Pickens County Library System.)

EASLEY PRESBYTERIAN CHURCH. Organized on May 9, 1886, the congregation first met in the Easley Academy with only 17 charter members. In 1887, the first building was constructed in the same location where the larger church stands today. (Photograph courtesy of Dub Fortner.)

Four

Past, Present, and Future

I am not afraid of tomorrow, for I have seen yesterday and I love today.

—William Allen White

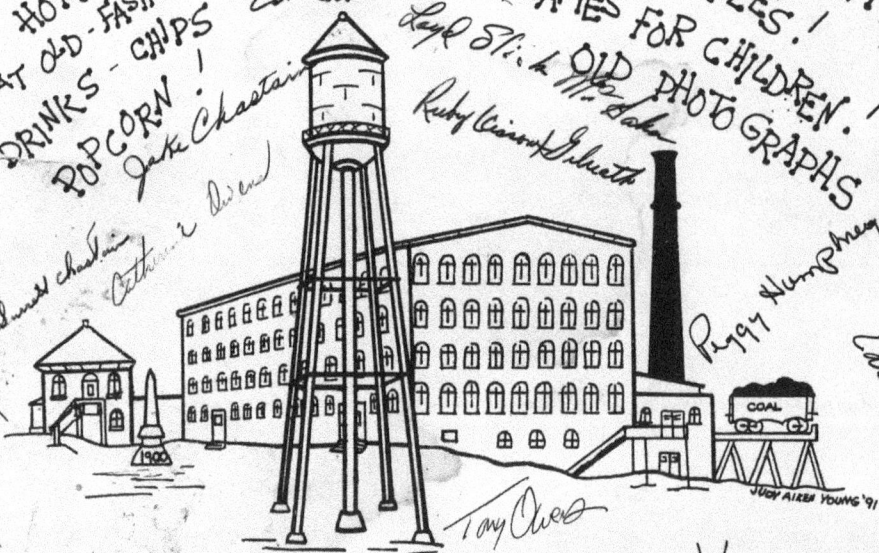

MILL REUNION FLYER. No single line of text or photograph more perfectly encapsulates the feeling of Easley's connection of the past, present, and future. This flyer, signed by festivalgoers, was taken from the program of the 1991 Easley Cotton Mill reunion. Multiple generations gathered to celebrate their history, discuss their current lives, and begin planning for upcoming reunions. Easley Mill is not the only mill community that hosts such reunions. Maybe Thomas Wolfe did say that one could never go home again, but the author's grandfather was of the belief that you should never forget where you came from. (Photograph courtesy of the Owens family.)

PICKENSVILLE. Before Easley was Easley and the county seat was Pickens, there was Pickensville. All that is left of that village is this South Carolina Heritage Corridor marker showing where Pickensville once was. It has now been enfolded by Easley and its name taken by the next town over. Gone but not forgotten, Pickensville brought farmers to the region and gave birth to the idea of a railroad in this area. (Photograph by B. Owens.)

WELCOME TO EASLEY. As Easley continues to prosper in size, population, and industry, the city strives to provide every possible advantage for its citizens and visitors, from the smallest details like the welcome signs, to an ever-expanding infrastructure of police, fire, and city services. (Photograph by B. Owens.)

THE WATER TOWER. The first municipal water tower to be erected in the 1960s proudly bears the name of Easley. A new water tower was constructed in 2007–2008 to supplement the original tower because of the city's growth. (Photograph courtesy of Newell Hester.)

School House, Easley, S. C.

THE ACADEMY IN 1900. The first official school in Easley taught many of the prominent citizens mentioned in these pages. That school paved the way for a network of elementary schools, a middle school, and a high school. (Photograph courtesy of Newell Hester.)

PROGRESS. After the new high school was built, the former Easley High School went through several incarnations, including time as a sewing hall. In the mid-2000s, Dave Watson echoed the pioneering spirit of Easley's forefathers by turning the empty building into luxury condos, helping to revitalize the historic downtown area. (Photograph by B. Owens.)

BREAKING GROUND. The Easley High School Band was on hand, along with school district members, chamber of commerce members, and future students, to break ground on the site of the new Easley High School. Although the project was started in 2008, it will be several years before the large, state-of-the-art facility is completed. (Photograph courtesy of the Greater Easley Chamber of Commerce.)

FRIERSON'S DRUG STORE. A staple in the downtown business district since 1924, this drugstore has undergone few changes over the years. This shot from the 1940s illustrates the unique architecture of the corner buildings of the time. Notice the triangle-shaped awning created by the roof extending to the corner post. (Photograph courtesy of the Pickens County Library System.)

FRIERSON'S TODAY. Having filled millions of prescriptions, Frierson's is still a small-town family drugstore. The only things that have really changed are the enclosure of the front of the building and the names of the doctors writing the prescriptions. (Photograph by B. Owens.)

DOWNTOWN BOUTIQUES. The revitalization of downtown includes the same buildings being put to different uses. Cafés, antiques shops, and specialty clothing stores line this side of the tracks facing Pickens. (Photograph courtesy of the Pickens County Library System.)

SHOPPING IN THE 1930s. This is the same view of Main Street and the shopping district in the 1930s. The Lyric Theatre was in the middle of the action. Today Easley's theater is on the Highway 123 Bypass. (Photograph courtesy of the Pickens County Library System.)

A DIFFERENT VIEW. This view of Main Street in the 1930s looks toward what would one day become Highway 93, which merges into Highway 123. The latter would eventually become a major travel corridor and the city's commerce district. The citizens of town then probably could not imagine the changes to come. (Photograph courtesy of the Pickens County Library System.)

STARTING SMALL. The official Greater Easley Chamber of Commerce was chartered after World War II in 1947. Beginning small, Jack Ragsdale and a few other businessmen set up shop in this tiny building on Main Street. (Photograph courtesy of Dub Fortner.)

PENDLETON STREET. Certainly no longer Table Rock Road, Pendleton Street constitutes one half of the largest intersection in downtown. One can still see the tracks in the distance across Main Street and the same brick buildings that have lined Pendleton Street since the beginning of the 20th century. (Photograph courtesy of Newell Hester.)

DOWNTOWN'S MAIN INTERSECTION. This is a current view of the intersection that was the main artery of the small 1-square-mile town with a depot for a heart. To get anywhere in Easley, this intersection will probably be used. One can see the tracks in the foreground in approximately the same spot as the old depot. (Photograph courtesy of the Pickens County Library System.)

LUKE'S TAXI. From this angle, one gets a different perspective of Pendleton Street toward Main Street. In 1965, Pendleton Street was a vital part of the downtown-area business district. This is a statement toward the economic boom felt in Easley and especially the downtown area until the early 1980s, when most business migrated to the Highway 123 Bypass. Today the revitalization of downtown has brought many businesses back to Pendleton Street. (Photograph courtesy of Dub Fortner.)

KEEPING TIME. The clock tower in Old Market Square marks the passage of time for the town of Easley. Having recently undergone renovations, Old Market Square is being updated to provide weekly events for the citizens of Easley as well as parking for the shopping district. (Photograph by B. Owens.)

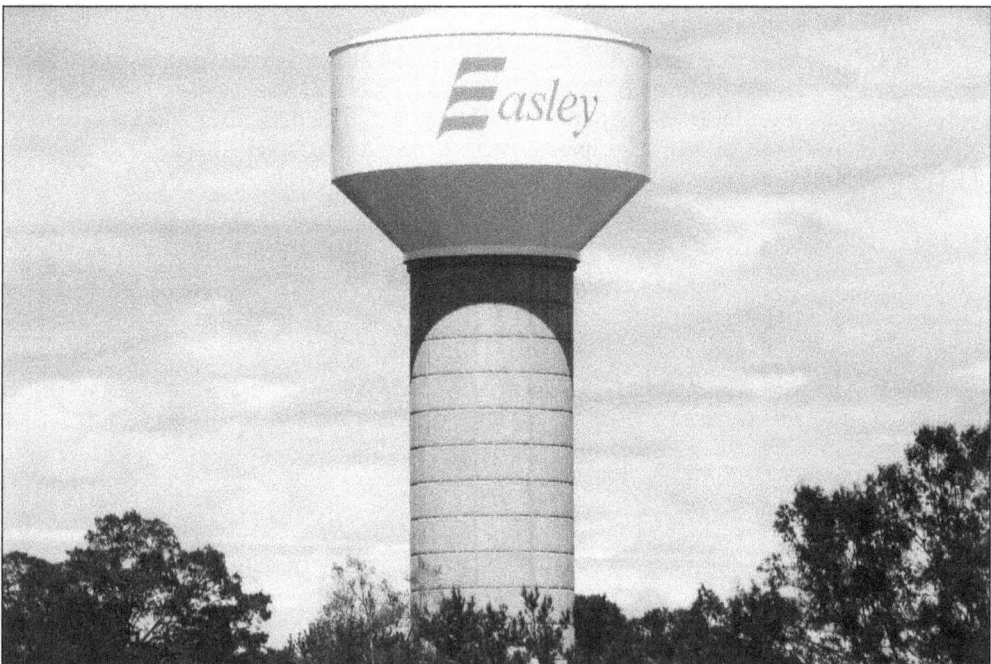

KEEPING UP. In 2007, the City of Easley and Easley Combined Utilities erected a new water tower to serve the citizens of Easley. (Photograph courtesy of Kent Dykes.)

RECREATION. First there was Pope Field Park, and then there was an old armory building that had been commandeered for the Easley Recreation Gymnasium. Now Easley boasts a 46-acre sports complex that plays host to the Little League World Series. (Photograph courtesy of the Greater Easley Chamber of Commerce.)

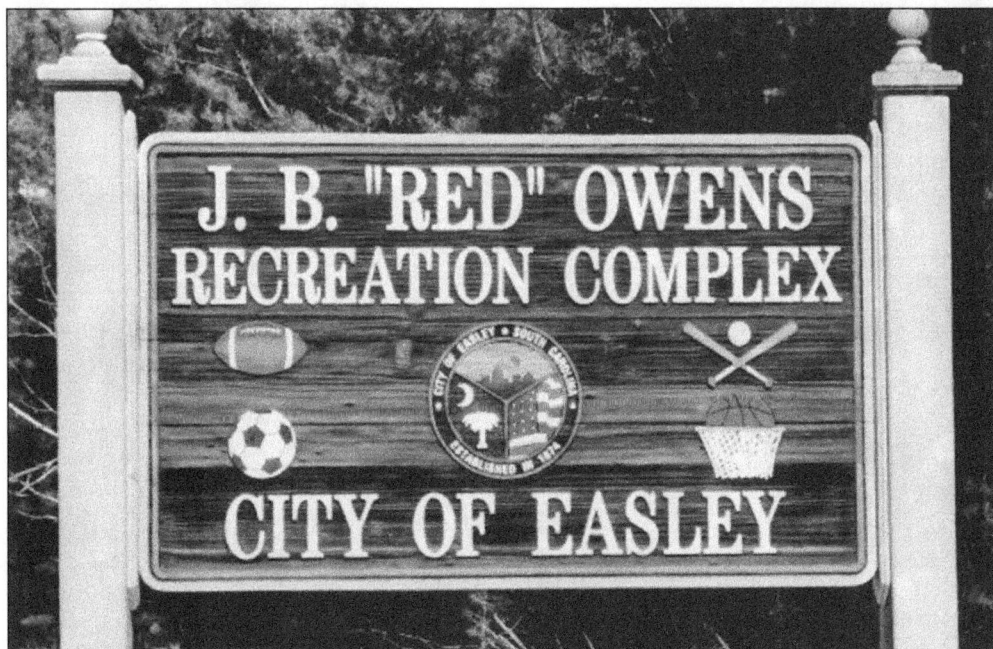

THE PARK. The park, named after J. B. "Red" Owens, includes football fields, soccer fields, baseball and softball fields, disc golf, walking trails, and the new Larry D. Bagwell Gymnasium, which has three basketball courts. (Photograph by B. Owens.)

J. B. "RED" OWENS. Shown here in his U.S. Army uniform, Red was instrumental in the development of athletics and recreation in Easley, as well as being a civic leader. A city councilman for 28 years, he was also mayor pro tem, an assistant coach for the Easley High School football team, and the director of Easley Cotton Mill recreation. Red was also active in Glenwood mill athletics (where he was also director of human resources), and he played both semi-professional baseball and football in his youth. (Photograph courtesy of the Owens family.)

BIG LEAGUE WORLD SERIES. The Big League World Series champions for the fourth year in a row in 2007, the South Carolina District 1 team played against teams from all over the world at the J. B. "Red" Owens Recreation Complex. In 2007, ESPN broadcast the championship game, drawing international attention to the small town. (Photograph courtesy of the City of Easley, Easley Recreation Department.)

NEW GYM. The latest addition to the J. B. "Red" Owens Complex is a three-court gymnasium. Named for local athletic hero and now mayor Larry D. Bagwell, the facility includes meeting rooms, concessions stands, and an arcade. (Photograph courtesy of the Greater Easley Chamber of Commerce.)

EASLEY HIGH SCHOOL FOOTBALL TEAM. Six seniors on the Easley High School Football team pose for a picture during their final season in 1935. From left to right are (first row) Ferber Whitmire, Kirt Norton, and Jack Ragsdale; (second row) Bill Furman, Paul Rampey, and Sam Boggs. (Photograph courtesy of Jack Ragsdale.)

CHEERLEADING. High school sports are not what they used to be. Here is a cheerleading squad from the 1940s in front of the original wooden gymnasium. Among those pictured are Annie Bell Turpin Wyatt, Dot Hagood Grantham, Katherine Fant, Cannie Hamilton, Mellicent White, Elizabeth Campbell, Claire Sims, Peggy Mulkey, and Jeanette Carman. (Photograph courtesy of Dub Fortner.)

JOE'S ICE CREAM PARLOR. Serving Easley's sweet tooth and hamburger cravings for more than 30 years, Joe's is a local stop for almost everyone in town. In New York City, there is Carnegie's Deli; in Spartanburg, South Carolina there is the Beacon; and in Easley, there is Joe's. (Photograph by B. Owens.)

PALMETTO BAPTIST HEALTH EASLEY. In 1947, Dr. W. M. Whitesides and Johnny Roper approached the Easley Rotary Club with the desire to build a hospital for the citizens of Easley. Ellison McKissick Sr., Gertrude Hagood Mathews, Julian Wyatt, R. C. McCall, and Roper made substantial donations, and with the help of the South Carolina Baptist Convention, the building was complete in 1958. Originally, it was called the Easley Hospital. Through various donations and after being integrated into a larger health care system, it became the Palmetto Health Baptist Easley Hospital, which has grown in size along with the town and has served its citizens for more than 50 years. (Photograph by B. Owens.)

GERTRUDE MATHEWS. Gertrude Hagood Mathews was a member of the prominent Hagood family. She donated time and money to churches, schools, and libraries. One of her most notable donations, however, was to the building of a hospital in Easley. She and others were of the belief that Easley had grown in wealth and population, and should have a proper facility to take care of its sick and injured citizens. (Photograph courtesy of the Pickens County Library System.)

IT IS STILL THE MOUNTAIN VIEW. No longer housing weary travelers fresh from the train, the Mountain View Hotel Antiques building houses memories. On the second floor, in what was once a rental room, is a mini-museum, and the building still holds its original charm and distinctive roofline. (Photograph by B. Owens.)

THIS IS THE MOUNTAIN VIEW. In the Easley area, Table Rock is one of the most pristine, beautiful, and visited tourist locations in South Carolina. One can see why the hotel took the name Mountain View. Taken in 1889, this is one of the earliest photographs of the mountain and the clubhouse. (Photograph courtesy of Newell Hester.)

TABLE ROCK CLUBHOUSE. A closer view of the Table Rock Clubhouse in the early 1900s shows how small the original wooden structure was and how pristine the countryside was at that time. Nathan Keith enjoys the solitude. Now a state park, the clubhouse has been replaced by a large, two-story, stone clubhouse surrounded by a beautifully preserved forest and amazing views of the surrounding mountains and foothills. (Photograph courtesy of Newell Hester.)

THE LIBRARY. This library and sign memorializes a local officer, Capt. Kimberly Hampton, a helicopter pilot who was killed in Iraq. The Easley branch of the Pickens County Library System has grown tremendously since the first bookmobile of donated items. This high-tech institution boasts a state-of-the-art computer lab, a computer indexing system, a local history room, meeting rooms, study rooms, and a coffeehouse. (Photographs by B. Owens.)

THE ORIGINAL EASLEY LIBRARY. Built in the 1960s, this small building served the needs of the citizens and children of Easley for more than three decades. However, as the town grew, the downtown location left no room for expansion, so a new three-story building was built, and the old library has become part of the commercial district downtown. (Photograph courtesy of the Pickens County Library System.)

BUSY TOWN. By the 1950s, one can see how busy the downtown area had become, even at night. Back then, Easley was said to "roll up the sidewalk at 9:00 p.m." by the locals, although there was still plenty of cruising along the Pendleton Street drag. Today, because of the downtown revitalization, this scene of a bustling nightlife is becoming familiar once again. (Photograph courtesy of Dub Fortner.)

THE LAW ENFORCEMENT CENTER. This new law enforcement center stands beside the city hall along the track on West Main Street. Now far too large to be housed inside city hall, the Easley Police Department has grown in technology, employees, and skill. The department has been keeping watch over the citizens of Easley since 1910. (Photograph by B. Owens.)

NON–CITY SPONSORED FUN. In the 1950s, as the Highway 123 corridor was just beginning to become a major business district, a bowling alley was built that stood alone along the miles of the corridor. It was extremely popular and was filled every weekend. (Photograph courtesy of the Pickens County Library System.)

STRIP MALLS. Now the bowling alley is part of a strip mall, as are many other businesses that grew up around the building. As the textile industry faded and the downtown area fell into disrepair, the town's economic focus switched to the acres of land that lined the highway. (Photograph by B. Owens.)

CALHOUN MEMORIAL HIGHWAY, OR HIGHWAY 123. Perhaps this photograph, more than any other, shows the blatant and unrelenting growth that Easley has undergone during the past 130 years. From this perspective, one can see the development of the highway toward Clemson, South Carolina. (Photograph by B. Owens.)

A FAR CRY. This small restaurant in the Glenwood mill village area is believed to be that mill's original store. It has been made into a café multiple times over the years without much renovation to the facade. With all the restaurants that have sprung up on the bypass, many continue to gather at this old café for lunch. (Photograph by B. Owens.)

MAIN STREET. EASLEY, S. C.
SHOWING BUSINESS SECTION AND SOUTHERN (MAIN LINE) DEPOT.

ONE LAST LOOK. These two photographs provide a final look at the downtown, railroad, and depot of yesteryear. In the above photograph, the depot is seen to the left on Main Street along with the famed Mountain View Hotel. The juxtaposition of these two photographs proves the lasting nature of the past through the indestructible and continued rebirth of the Mountain View, while at the same time reminding us of how quickly certain aspects of the past can fade. The depot no longer serves the public, and only freight trains buzz through downtown today. (Above, photograph courtesy of the Pickens County Library System; below, photograph courtesy of Dub Fortner.)

THE END OF AN ERA. The depot that gave life to Easley outlived its own usefulness and was razed in the 1960s to provide a clearer roadway. The destruction was quite controversial at the time and continues to be to this day. Many believe that the history of the building as a symbol of the town deserved to be preserved. (Photograph courtesy of Dub Fortner.)

THE DOODLE STATION. Those who wished for the preservation of the old depot may be getting the next best thing. The Doodle Station was built on almost the exact location of the original depot. Its name honors the history of the town and the railroad that gave it life. Of course, no trains will be stopping there because it is a unique shopping center. The builders did try to pay tribute to the past through the architecture and mementos found throughout the buildings. (Photograph by B. Owens.)

SAYING GOODBYE. After the depot was demolished, railroad enthusiasts included Easley along the route of the final steam-engine run. Even in the early 1980s, many turned out to catch a glimpse of that link to the past. (Photograph courtesy of Dub Fortner.)

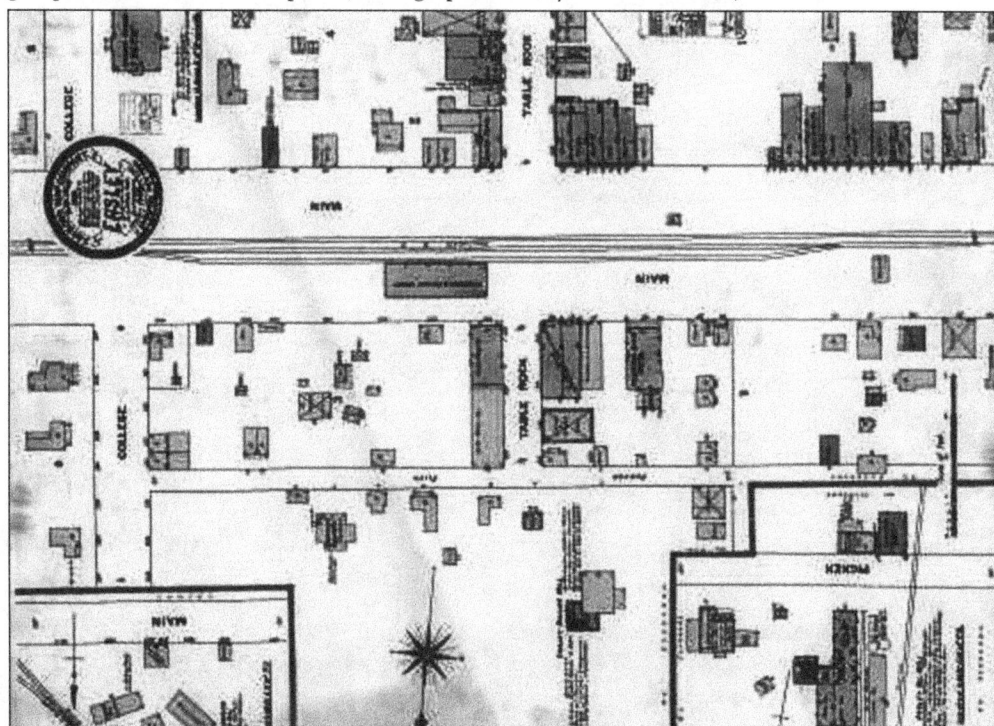

AN EARLY MAP. This map of Easley depicts the entire town in the 1880s. The 1-square-mile tract of town shows the depot, Table Rock Road (which would become Pendleton Street), and Main Street. From the 1800s to today, Easley has grown to a population of more than 28,000 in a city with all the modern amenities. (Photograph courtesy of the Pickens County Library System.)

HEADED OUT OF TOWN. There is no more depot, no more mills, and no more passenger trains—nothing left of the heart of this town but the railroad tracks. Might one look at this from a different perspective? This could be a photograph of Easley's old tracks leading into a limitless future. As long as what was is remembered and what is now is celebrated, then what will be is up to the citizens of Easley. The daily call of the train whistle heard throughout town is not the haunting sound of the past but a rally cry for Easley to follow into the future. (Photograph by B Owens.)

BIBLIOGRAPHY

Coke, Carol L. *Back Country of Old Pickens District*. Pickens, SC: 2002.

Forest Acres/MicKissick Quest Program. *Pickensville-Easley History*. Easley, SC: A Press, 1989.

McCravy, John R. *The History of Easley, South Carolina*. Easley, SC.

McFall, Pearl Smith. *It Happened in Pickens County*. Pickens, SC: The Sentinel Press, 1959.

Pendleton District Historical and Recreational Commission. *Pickens County History: A Teacher's Workbook*. Pendleton, SC: Pendleton District Historical and Recreational Commission.

Rogers, Harold, ed. *Pickens County Souvenir Program*. Pickens, SC: The Pickens County Centennial Commission, 1968.

Sheriff, Anne G., ed. *Black History in Pickens District, South Carolina*. Easley, SC: 1991.

The Easley Progress. Easley, SC: 1968.

INDEX

Visit us at
arcadiapublishing.com

....

www.ingramcontent.com/pod-product-compliance
Lightning Source LLC
Chambersburg PA
CBHW080623110426

42813CB00006B/1592